hello goodbye

a journey through life

Erin Yun

for all we welcome

and all we let go

as a child I say

hello
world

hello
kind hearts

hello

little wonders

hello

sunflowers

hello

honesty

hello
beautiful days

hello

mom

as an adult I say

hello

ambition

INVESTING
STRATEGIES
INVESTING STRATEGIE
THE HOMEBUILDER'S GUIDE
PATHWAYS TO SUCCESS
CAREER DEVELOPMENT
MASTERING
PEOPLE SKILLS
II
MASTERING PEOPLE SKILLS

hello
proving

hello
applause

hello
busy mornings

hello
expectations

hello

more

hello
endless days

now I say

goodbye
clutter

goodbye
rushing

goodbye
performing

goodbye
anger

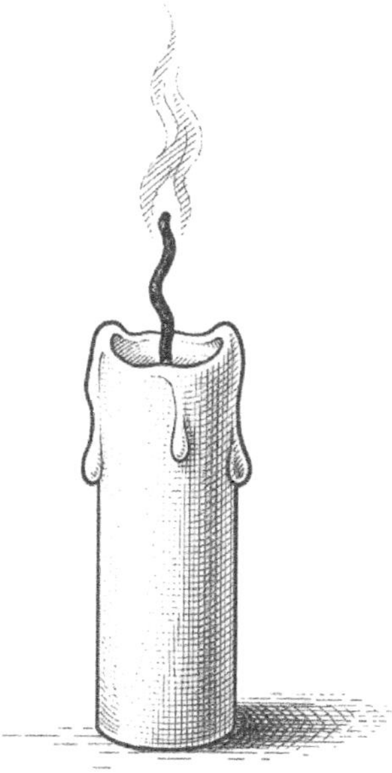

goodbye
wanting more

WELCOME

hello
peace

hello
morning light

hello
garden path

hello
memory

hello
enough

hello
home

hello
self

The story continues.

About the Author

Erin Yun writes quiet, reflective pieces,
often about giving, habits,
and relationships.

cloudpress.site

Made in the USA
Coppell, TX
05 June 2026

78999820R00038